THE JOY OF
CHICKENS

THE JOY OF
CHICKENS

DENNIS NOLAN

Prentice-Hall, Inc., Englewood Cliffs, New Jersey

Printed in the United States of America

Prentice-Hall International, Inc., London
Prentice-Hall of Australia, Pty. Ltd., North Sydney
Prentice-Hall of Canada, Ltd., Toronto
Prentice-Hall of India Private Ltd., New Delhi
Prentice-Hall of Japan, Inc., Tokyo
Prentice-Hall of Southeast Asia Pte. Ltd., Singapore
Whitehall Books Limited, Wellington, New Zealand

10 9 8 7 6 5 4 3 2 1

Prentice-Hall, Inc., Englewood Cliffs, New Jersey

Nolan, Dennis.
   The joy of chickens.

   SUMMARY: Discusses the history, physical characteristics, and habits of various breeds of chickens.
   1. Chickens—Juvenile literature.   2. Chicken breeds—Juvenile literature.   [1. Chickens.   2. Chicken breeds]   I. Title.
SF487.5.N64   636.5   80-18963
ISBN 0-13-511659-7

"Who is he who sets the world in motion, a mighty speared and lordly god? It is Parodaro, the cock that lifts up his voice against the mighty dawn."—*Ancient Sacred Book of the Parsees*

ACKNOWLEDGMENTS

I would like to thank my neighbors, Don and Mary Goold, Erv and Lee Springs, and John and Ruth Daros, for introducing me to the world of chickens. I would like to thank the members of the Pacific Poultry Breeders Association and the many fanciers who allowed me to photograph their chickens, Frank Joseph, Ralph Marsh, Margaret Benton, Walt Leonard, Sandra Warnken, Dennis Hanna, Gary Wilson, Diane Williams, Bob and Kathy Jarvis, Edd Abblett, Ron Giovanetti, Bonnie Cook, Julie Uhouse, Joyce Clover, Alan Feagley, Rod Ridnour, Barbara Ranaletti, Andrew Banyai, Allan Watts, Angela Cocker, Brian Cincotta, Russ Beach, William Fuher, Jill Sallee, Jim and Bonnie Sallee, Ed Medzian, Howard Goehring, Russ Cocker, Richard Barger, Scott Carrington, Gary Shirley, and Bruce Sherman. I would also like to thank Francine Bradley and Frank X. Ogasawara of the Dept. of Avian Science, U.C. Davis, Joe Williamson, Michael Gaston, Richard Stiller, Rod Bean, Maxine Harmon, and Evelyn Helmer for helping to make this book complete. And a special thanks to my editor, Ellen Roberts, for seeing this project through.

LIST OF ILLUSTRATIONS

For Susie and Andy

WHAT IS A CHICKEN?

It may come with stripes, spots, patches, one color, two colors, or a rainbow of colors. It may weigh as much as 14 pounds or as little as 1½ pounds. It may grow a 30-foot tail or no tail at all. It might be tall and skinny or short and fat or have five toes instead of four. It may lay white eggs or brown eggs or even blue eggs. But no matter what the shape or color, it is always that same clucking, pecking, scratching, egg-laying member of the barnyard, the chicken.

Almost everyone knows the chicken. It is probably the most common bird in the world. There are more chickens on this earth than there are humans, and its history is as long and interesting as human history.

Chickens are raised for meat, for eggs, and for their beauty. There are over 50 distinct breeds of chicken today, and they all share one common ancestor, the Red Jungle Fowl of Ceylon.

1   *Red Jungle Fowl, male*

CHICKEN RELATIVES

The Red Jungle Fowl is one of four species of Jungle Fowl that live in the jungles of Southeast Asia. Actually, they are all members of the pheasant family. This group contains some of the most beautifully colored and patterned birds in the world. The delicate Golden Pheasant, the elegant Lady Amherst Pheasant, the common Ring-Necked Pheasant, and the proud Peacock are all part of this group, which is found throughout India, Tibet, and Indochina. The pheasant has traveled with people since before written history, and it was well-known in Ancient Greece and Rome. It has provided eggs and meat and has been praised for its beauty for centuries. The Jungle Fowl differs from all other pheasants in having a comb and wattles about the head and in its distinctively curved tail. It may still be found in the wild, living much the same as it did before man.

Other relatives of the Jungle Fowl include the common Quail, the Prairie Chicken, and the Turkey. Perhaps the closest relative of the chicken in both appearance and habit is the Guinea Fowl of Southern Africa. A strange-looking bird, the Guinea Fowl has long been raised for its delicious meat. The Helmeted Guinea Fowl, one of seven species, is typical of the rest. It is purplish-gray in color, spangled with small white spots, and its gaudy, white-and-red, featherless head is topped by a bony crest. Its harsh, earsplitting cackle has kept it from being raised on farms. Occasionally, however, a number are kept, like watchdogs, to warn other barnyard poultry of a threatening hawk or weasel. They are good flyers but usually prefer to run from danger.

2   *Helmeted Guinea Fowl*

A HISTORY OF CHICKENS

The history of chickens begins 75-million years ago with the first chicken-like bird. This bird roamed the forests of Southeastern Asia for centuries, eating small plants and insects and crowing at dawn. It is believed that primitive man began keeping chickens 10,000 years ago, for the eggs the hens would lay and for the meat they provided. The chicken was small, easy to care for and feed, hardy in all types of weather, and could easily travel with people wherever they went. The male chicken, called the cock, also provided mankind with one of its oldest sports, cockfighting, which helped spread the chicken around the world.

The chicken was well-known as a fighter in India in 3,000 B.C., and Persians used the chicken for fighting and as an object of sacrifice as early as 600 B.C. The chicken was also imported to Greece, where it decorated coins and official seals, and then to Rome, where it was admired for its bravery and usefulness. Cockfighting also spread eastward to China and Japan and throughout the Pacific Islands.

Gradually the Red Jungle Fowl was transformed into many distinct breeds. China concentrated on raising large, heavy chickens for eating, Japan turned its attention to raising many fancy varieties, and Europeans developed small, slender breeds for laying and fighting.

Egypt was the first country to produce eggs on a major scale. In 2,000 B.C., clay-brick incubators, capable of hatching 10,000 eggs at a time, were kept warm with simple wood fires. The Romans also raised chickens for their eggs, using marble nest eggs to induce the hens to lay. A law passed in Rome in 161 B.C. outlawed fattening a hen for the purpose of eating it. Some people continued to fatten their hens, however, using diets of lizard fat, barley meal, and cumin seed.

The Romans attached much superstition to the chicken, as did many other people of the world. Chicks refusing to leave their house in the morning were thought to foretell the coming of rain. If a sacred chicken ate heartily, it meant success of a military campaign. The right foot of a chicken brought good luck to its owner and its early morning crowing scared away the devil spirits of the night. By the fall of the Roman Empire, 476 A.D., the chicken was well-known throughout Europe, Asia, and Northern Africa.

During the Middle Ages and the Renaissance, cockfighting again became a popular pastime in Europe. King Henry VIII of England built a cockpit at Whitehall Palace, although he outlawed the sport for a while. It was made legal again for a time, and schoolboys brought their fighting cocks to school and used the classroom as an arena.

Spanish explorers brought chickens to America. The English, French, and Dutch brought more, but no chickens came over on the Mayflower.

Raising chickens on a large scale began in the mid-1800s with the invention of chicken wire to keep the chickens from straying. Better modes of transportation took chickens and eggs to market. Soon flocks of three- or four-thousand chickens were common. Improved food was made available for fatter and better laying hens. Today, raising chickens for meat and eggs is a big business, with over two-billion chickens in the United States alone. The common, commercial flock of hens may number one million and average 220 eggs, per chicken, per year.

FOLK TALES

The chicken has been the subject of many stories in many lands. Cock crowing and fighting have been used as examples of both vanity and courage. And the hen's care of her eggs and chicks has been used as an example of motherly love, while endless cackling and clucking have been used to represent the spreading of rumors. The chicken is one of the animals of the Chinese zodiac, symbolizing honor and merit. Aesop used chickens in a number of his fables, Chaucer immortalized two chickens named Chanticleer and Pertelote, and Rimsky-Korsakov made a golden chicken the central figure of his opera *Le Coq d'Or*. Nursery rhymes give us three popular chickens: the Little Red Hen, Henny-Penny, and Chicken Little. The famous goose that laid the golden egg was at first a chicken.

The chicken was also thought to have magical powers. In France, during the Middle Ages, a black chicken was used as a symbol of the devil. If a person took a black cock to a crossroads at midnight and yelled "Black chicken for sale" three times, it was said the devil would appear and buy the bird for a handful of gold.

3   Cockatrice

The Cockatrice was one of the most widely feared monsters of medieval Europe. It was only two feet long, but merely to look upon it meant sudden death. It was said to be born of a small, round egg laid by a seven-year-old cock. It was then hatched out after nine years by a toad. Described as being part chicken, part toad, and part snake, the Cockatrice grew in legend until it became the "King of Serpents." Its fiery eyes could kill anything it gazed upon; a mere glance could split rock and burn grass. The Cockatrice could turn fertile land into a desert and could poison the waters. The Cockatrice could only be killed by a weasel, its own reflection in a mirror, or the crowing of a cock. Medieval travelers were careful to carry a caged cock with them whenever journeying through unknown territory.

THE CHICKEN AND
THE EGG

All chickens begin life as an egg. A fertilized egg contains a yolk and a small embryo that weighs less than 1/100,000 of an ounce. If the egg is warmed by a hen, called a broody hen, or an incubator, it will hatch in twenty-one days. The temperature must stay at 100.5°F, and the eggs must occasionally be rotated. On the first day the tiny embryo already has the beginnings of a backbone, intestine, nervous system, and two small specks that will become eyes. On the second day the heart begins to beat, and by the third day the embryo can be seen with the naked eye. This is done by holding the egg up to a light, a process called candling. By the eighth day the embryo has feathers and is beginning to look like a chick. Near the end of the third week the chick begins to see light and to respond to sounds outside the shell; it weighs more than 150,000 times its original weight and completely fills the inside of the egg. On the twentieth day the chick breaks through the air sac and begins to breathe. The mother hen and chick cluck, chirp, and screech back and forth to each other as the chick prepares to break through the shell. On the twenty-first day the chick breaks the shell with the help of its egg tooth, a small, bony projection on its beak. It may take six hours to peck a ring around the eggshell and finally kick itself free.

After a couple of hours of resting and warming up, the chick is ready to begin searching for food. Many birds must depend on their parents for food during the first few weeks of life, but a baby chicken is ready to find food for itself immediately after hatching.

All baby chicks are covered with furry down feathers. By six weeks both young female chickens, called pullets, and young male chickens, called cockerels, have about 8,500 true feathers of a full-grown chicken. Combs and wattles appear at eight weeks of age.

When they are five months old, chickens start reproducing, and a hen may lay 1,000 eggs in a seven-year lifetime. The first chicken to lay more than 300 eggs a year was a hen named Lady Macduff, who laid 303 eggs in 1912.

Each year both hens and cocks molt, losing all of their feathers. It takes three months for new feathers to grow in, during which time the hen stops laying eggs.

4   *Rhode Island Red, chick and pullet*

5   *Rhode Island Red, female*

DIFFERENT BREEDS FOR DIFFERENT NEEDS

Chickens raised for commercial purposes can be divided into three groups: the egg producers, the meat chickens, and the dual-purpose breeds.

Most chicken breeds lay brown-shelled eggs, but white-shelled are the most popular. The best-known egg producer is the White Leghorn, which originated in Italy and was once called the Italiana. A White Leghorn hen weighs an average of 4 pounds and lays 220 to 240 white-shelled eggs each year, weighing an average of 58 grams each. By comparison, an ostrich lays the largest egg of any bird, weighing 1,400 grams, while the hummingbird lays the smallest at ½ gram. The largest chicken egg on record is a 320-gram egg laid by a White Leghorn.

Dual-purpose chickens are raised for both meat and eggs. The Rhode Island Red and the Barred Plymouth Rock are two popular dual-purpose varieties. The Rhode Island Red is an American creation descended from the Red Malay Game chicken brought to the United States in the early 1800s. The Barred Plymouth Rock is also an American breed, developed in the 1860s by Pastor Upham of Connecticut. The Cornish is probably the most popular meat chicken. Named for the county in England where it originated, the Cornish is a mixture of the Aseel, Malay, and English Game. Once called the Indian Game, the Cornish is massive in appearance, averaging eight to ten pounds in weight, and has close-fitting feathers and almost nonexistent comb and wattles. The popular Rock-Cornish Game hen is a cross between a Cornish and a White Plymouth Rock.

6   *White Leghorn, female*

7 *Barred Plymouth Rock, female*

8   *White-Laced Red Cornish, male*

CHICKENS TO LOOK AT

A number of chicken breeds are raised strictly for exhibition, with no concern for their economic value, and most are of a dwarf, or bantam, variety.

The word bantam comes from the Bantam district in Java, where small chickens were raised for centuries. The first ones were exported to Europe by the Dutch in 1700. Most chicken breeds today have a bantam variety, but some ornamental breeds are raised only as bantams. The average weight of an ornamental bantam is 1½ pounds.

The small rose-comb and beard of the Quail Belgian and the delicate cream and light-blue coloring of the feather-legged Porcelain Belgian are examples of the decorative qualities of this group. The Black Rose-Comb was once simply called the Black Bantam. It became a popular showbird in England, with its glossy, greenish-black plumage, its bright red rose-comb, and its large, white earlobes. The Hamburg, though its name is German, is actually from Holland. The English perfected the Silver-Spangled variety, once popular with both fanciers and commercial poultry breeders for their white-shelled eggs. They come in both large and bantam varieties.

9   *Quail Belgian Bantam, male, and Porcelain Belgian Bantam, female*

10   *Black Rose-Comb Bantam, male*

11 *Silver-Spangled Hamburg. male*

RAISING CHICKENS

The oldest chicken on record lived twenty-five years. The average life span of a chicken is seven years. Most egg-laying chickens are past their prime at a year and a half, at which time they become stewing chickens. A meat chicken becomes a broiler at eight weeks of age.

Most commercial poultry businesses are housed in huge buildings. Their laying hens are kept in cages, and their incubators hatch out 50,000 eggs or more at a time. Feeding, watering, and preparation for market are all automated tasks. The United States alone turns out three billion broilers a year and keeps 300 million hens laying. On a small scale, a half-dozen hens can lay enough eggs for a family most of the year.

An area of ground, fenced in by chicken wire, keeps predators out and chickens in, while a henhouse provides a place to sleep and lay. Small breeds, such as the Mille Fleur Bantam, require very little care and are inexpensive to feed. Corn, wheat, barley, oats, and milo make up most chicken diets, with commercial feed adding minerals, vitamins, and antibiotics. Small plants, insects, slugs, and snails provide a feast for the chicken allowed to roam free.

12 *Mille Fleur Booted Bantam, male and female*

LAYERS AND FIGHTERS

The wide stance, long neck, and powerful body of the Old English Game is the result of thousands of years of breeding. Descended from the fighting cocks, the Old English reached its peak of popularity in England during the seventeenth and eighteenth centuries. Fights, or "mains," were advertised daily. Large sums of money were wagered, and rigid rules and regulations were followed. Combs and wattles were trimmed, or "dubbed," and steel spurs were attached to the legs. Many varieties were developed, including Polecats, Gingers, Custards, Mealy Grays, and the popular Black-Breasted Reds. Another variety called "Shakebags" was developed, the name referring to the bags carrying the cocks to the scene of the fight. They were then shaken into the "pit" to battle their opponents. The Shammo Japanese is similar to the Malay and other fighting breeds of Indochina and the Pacific Islands. The Shammo may stand over 30 inches high.

Built for strength and speed, the body of a fighter is slight and spare when compared to a modern meat chicken like the Wyandotte. A popular American breed, the Wyandotte is raised for both meat and eggs. The Silver-Laced variety is a product of crosses between Buff Cochins and Silver Sebrights, and Dark Brahmas and Silver-Spangled Hamburgs.

13   Old English Black-Breasted Red Game, male

14 Shammo Japanese. male

15   *Silver-Laced Wyandotte, male*

EAST AND WEST

The chickens of Asia were raised mainly for eating, and were heavy-bodied birds. The Black Langshan, named for a district near the Yangtze River in China, has typically feathered legs and weighs ten pounds. The Cochin and the Brahma, also from Asia, may weigh as much as 14 pounds when fully grown. The Brahma comes from India near the Brahma-pootra River. First shipped to America in 1846 from Shanghai, China, it was called the Gray Chittagong. Also known as "Lord of Creation," the Brahma has been used in the development of many new breeds of meat chicken.

Little is known of the ancestry of the South American chicken, the Araucana. It is bearded, rumpless, and is the only chicken that lays blue-shelled eggs. They are named for a Chilean Indian tribe. By the 1500's, the Araucana was well-established throughout South America. The last ruler of the Peruvian Inca tribe was named Atahualpa, which means chicken.

16   *Black Langshan, male*

17   *Rumpless Bearded Araucana, male and female*

18 *Light Brahma, male*

CHICKEN FEVER

The Cochin chicken of China arrived in England in 1845, setting off a "poultry-mania." A group of these huge, full-feathered birds was presented as a gift to Queen Victoria. They were described as being as large as ostriches and able to roar like lions. When they were first displayed in Birmingham, they impressed the public with their beauty, size, and gentle nature. Thousands of people became chicken fanciers overnight, eager to own the "Shanghai Fowl." Single Cochins sold for more than an average worker's yearly pay. Soon the Cochin craze settled down, but the raising of purebred poultry remained popular. The first Cochins in England were a Buff variety, but soon White, Black, and Partridge varieties were being bred. A bantam variety, once known as Pekin, was introduced in many color choices. The Cochins, full-sized and bantam, remain popular showbirds today.

19   *White Cochin, female*

20　Black Cochin Bantam, male

21   *White Cochin, male*

TOPKNOTS

The chicken with the feather-duster topknot is known as the Polish but does not come from Poland. It was first recorded in the Netherlands in the sixteenth century, where it was known as the Crested Dutch. It probably originated in Italy, a descendant of the Polvera from Padua. Charles Darwin classified all crested fowl as "crested or polish," possibly referring to the "poll" of feathers that forms the topknot. In males this consists of long, narrow feathers that fall evenly around the head, while the female's topknot is held high and round. Promise of a future crest can be seen on the chicks. Many color varieties exist, White-Crested Blacks being the most popular. Other varieties are White-Crested Blue, Buff, Silver, Gold, and White. They may be clean faced or bearded, full-sized or bantam. The Polish was once a popular egg-laying breed, but it is now kept mainly as an ornamental showbird.

22   *White-Crested Black Polish, male*

23   *Buff-Laced Bearded Polish, male and female*

24   *White-Crested Blue Polish Bantam, female*

SLEEK AND SHOWY

After the outlawing of cockfighting and the popularization of the poultry show, the Game Fowl underwent some dramatic changes. No longer bred for power and ferocity, the Game Fowl became a small, slender showbird of delicate proportions. Long neck and legs, short feathers, and a slight, compact body were all requirements of this new chicken called the Modern Game. The comb and wattles are dubbed to add to the high "station" or stance of the Modern Game.

The tiny Japanese is one of the ornamental bantam breeds. With its large comb and wattles, short legs, and long full tail, it is almost opposite in appearance to the Modern Game. The tail feathers, or sickles, are carried high and forward, almost touching the head. Many color varieties exist in this ancient breed whose ancestry can be traced back many centuries in Japan.

The Sebright is another of the ornamental bantam breeds. It originated in England, the result of thirty years of breeding by Sir John Sebright. The feathering of male and female are exactly alike, a rare occurrence in poultry.

25 Birchen Modern Game, male

26   *White Japanese Bantam, male*

27   Silver Sebright Bantam, male and female

SILKIES AND FRIZZLES

The chicken with the soft, powder-puff look is the Silkie. The feathers are not webbed and give the appearance of soft fur. Such "fur" and the deep-purple skin of the Silkie make it unlike any other breed of poultry. Silkies have been known for centuries, but their origin is not clear. Many were imported from Singapore where they were prized not for their flesh or egg laying but for their setting and brooding qualities. Used mainly for hatching pheasant eggs, Silkies make wonderful parents. Their silky-feathered legs, topknots, and comical appearance make them a favorite among fanciers of exhibition fowl. The original Silkies were all white, but there are now Black, Buff, and Blue varieties.

Another curiously feathered chicken is the Frizzle from India. The feathers curl backward, giving a ruffled appearance. It has been bred with other breeds of chicken, with some interesting results. Frizzled feathers look best on full-feathered breeds such as the Cochin.

28   *White Silkie, male*

29   *Buff Frizzle Cochin Bantam, male*

30   *Buff Silkie, Female*

TALE OF A TAIL

Perhaps the most remarkable of all chicken breeds is the Onagadori, the long-tailed fowl of Japan. Rare and beautiful, these birds have been raised in Japan for over three hundred years. Their history is well documented, beginning in 1655 with Riemon Takechi, who bred the bird for its tail feathers. These feathers were used to decorate ceremonial spear blades used in processions. Today the chickens are raised by less than two-dozen fanciers on the island of Shikoku in Japan. Government decree has made the Onagadori a Special Natural Commemorated Object.

The Onagadori's extremely long tail is nurtured for years with patience and care. The feathers of the tail region—the sickles, saddle, and covert—grow about three feet per year. These feathers do not molt but are kept throughout a lifetime. In order to ensure the greatest possible growth, the Onagadori must be kept in specially built boxes that restrict movement and allow a place for the tail to be coiled and safe from harm. If the birds were allowed to run free or mate, their tails would break. Carefully supervised periods of exercise and exhibition at poultry shows are the only moments of freedom in a prize Onagadori's life.

The Onagadori has been bred in three color varieties: Black and White, Red and Black, and All White. Only the males grow the long tails, which commonly measure 20 feet or more. One champion Onagadori was measured at 34.8 feet, truly a most amazing achievement.

31   *Black and White Onagadori, male*

ODDS AND ENDS

There are 56 breeds of standard chickens and many more nonstandard breeds and varieties. The Flemish Cuckoo, Owl-Bearded Dutch, German Creeper, Bearded Thuringian, Sicilian Buttercup, Siberian Feather-Footed, and Transylvanian Naked-Neck belong to this latter group. Chickens of both standard and nonstandard breeds may have single, rose, pea, walnut, V-shaped, buttercup, or strawberry combs. Their feathers may be laced, penciled, barred, stippled, spangled, or mottled.

Some chicken breeds may be traced back thousands of years, while others are relatively new. The offspring of two different breeds of chickens is called a hybrid, which may be crossed for better eggs, more delicious meat, or simply for the formation of a new and interesting breed of chicken. The results can be both beautiful and bizarre.

The chicken inhabits every continent except Antarctica. It is known as Das Huhn in German, Moa Hiwa in Hawaiian, Gai in Chinese, Pollo in Italian, Kuku in Swahili, Kuritsa in Russian, Gallina in Spanish, and Niwatori in Japanese. It is the state bird of Rhode Island and Delaware and the national bird of France.

Chickens have appeared on the painted walls of Egyptian tombs, on coins of ancient Greece, and on weather vanes around the world. It has been determined that yellow-orange is their favorite color, and scientists have separated their language into 20 different calls. Farmers everywhere know that a cock's crow signals the beginning of a new day.

Chickens have been bred in an infinite and dazzling array of sizes, shapes, colors, and patterns. Whether proud, fierce, comical, plain, or fancy, it is always a delight to hear and a pleasure to behold a chicken.

32   Hybrid, male